Dear Parent:

Buckle up! You are about to join your child on a very exciting journey. The destination? Independent reading!

Road to Reading will help you and your child get there. The program offers books at five levels, or Miles, that accompany children from their first attempts at reading to successfully reading on their own. Each Mile is paved with engaging stories and delightful artwork.

Getting Started
For children who know the alphabet and are eager to begin reading
• easy words   • fun rhythms   • big type   • picture clues

Reading With Help
For children who recognize some words and sound out others with help
• short sentences   • pattern stories   • simple plotlines

Reading On Your Own
For children who are ready to read easy stories by themselves
• longer sentences   • more complex plotlines   • easy dialogue

First Chapter Books
For children who want to take the plunge into chapter books
• bite-size chapters   • short paragraphs   • full-color art

Chapter Books
For children who are comfortable reading independently
• longer chapters   • occasional black-and-white illustrations

There's no need to hurry through the Miles. Road to Reading is designed without age or grade levels. Children can progress at their own speed, developing confidence and pride in their reading ability no matter what their age or grade.

So sit back and enjoy the ride—every Mile of the way!

To Cody and Rachel
who always want a ride
B.G.

For Boo, my friend...
C.N.

Library of Congress Cataloging-in-Publication Data
Gordh, Bill.
Want a ride? / by Bill Gordh ; illustrated by Carol Nicklaus.
   p.   cm. — (Road to reading.   Mile 2)
Summary: A series of smaller and smaller animals plays tricks on each other but
it is Ant, the very smallest animal, that plays the best trick of all.
ISBN 0-307-26204-9 (pbk.)
[1. Animals—Fiction.]   I. Nicklaus, Carol, ill.   II. Title.
III. Series.
PZ7.G6485Wan 1998
[E]—dc21   98-12755
                                                                   CIP
                                                                   AC

A GOLDEN BOOK • New York
Golden Books Publishing Company, Inc. New York, New York 10106

ISBN: 0-307-26204-9
                                                     A MCMXCVIII

Want a Ride?

by Bill Gordh
illustrated by Carol Nicklaus

Crocodile was the first
to play the trick.

She glided
down the river
until she saw Dog.

She asked Dog,
"Want a ride?
Want a ride
across the river
on my back?"

Dog said, "Okay,"
and got right on.

In the middle of the river
Crocodile sank.

Up, up, up
swam Dog.
He did not like
Crocodile's trick
one bit.

Dog walked along
the river
until he saw Cat.

Dog said,
"Want a ride?
Want a ride
across the river
on my back?"

Cat said, "Sure,"
and got right on.

Dog jumped into the river.
In the middle of the river
Dog sank.

Down, down, down
he went.

Up, up, up
swam Cat.

She did not like
Dog's trick
one bit.

The next day Cat
played the trick
on Frog.

The day after that
Frog played the trick
on Mouse.

Mouse played the trick
on Beetle.

Beetle played the trick on Ant.

Ant wanted
to play the trick.

She looked around.
"Who's smaller than me?"
But there was no one smaller
than ant.

Then Ant saw Crocodile
on the river bank.
Crocodile was having a picnic.

Ant said,
"Want a ride?
Want a ride
across the river
on my back?"

Crocodile stopped chewing.
"What did you say?"

Ant said it again.
"Want a ride?
Want a ride
across the river
on my back?"

Crocodile said, "Sure,"
and got right on.

Crocodile slid into the river.
She was thinking,
"Ha! That poor little ant
down under me!"

In the middle of the river
Crocodile looked back.

Ant was still
on the river bank.
Ant was eating
Crocodile's picnic!